Plants and Animals

by Debbie Allen

Glenview, Illinois
Boston, Massachusetts
Chandler, Arizona
Upper Saddle River, New Jersey

Photographs

Every effort has been made to secure permission and provide appropriate credit for photographic material.
The publisher deeply regrets any omission and pledges to correct errors called to its attention in subsequent editions.

Unless otherwise acknowledged, all photographs are the property of Pearson Education, Inc.

Photo locators denoted as follows: Top (T), Center (C), Bottom (B), Left (L), Right (R), Background (Bkgd)

Opener: Jupiter Images; 2 (B) Dave King/©DK Images; 4 (B) ©Martine Oger/Shutterstock; 5 (B) ©Peter Arnold,
Inc./Alamy Images, (T) Thinkstock; 8 (Inset) ©Casey K. Bishop/Shutterstock, (B) ©pjcross/Shutterstock; 10 (B) Jupiter
Images; 12 (BL) ©Elena Elisseeva/Shutterstock, (BR) ©Iurii Konoval/Shutterstock; 13 (BR) ©Bill Ross/Corbis, (BL)
©David Young-Wolff/PhotoEdit; 14 (B) ©Vaida/Shutterstock; 15 (B) Mike Dunning/©DK Images; FP2 (TCL) ©Lightworks
Media/Alamy Images, (TL) ©Masterfile Royalty-Free, (BR) ©Vaida/Shutterstock, (BL) Jupiter Images; FP6 (B) ©Martine
Oger/Shutterstock.

ISBN-13: 978-0-328-61717-3
ISBN-10:   0-328-61717-2

6 7 8 9 10 V0FL 14 13

Living Things

Plants are living things.

Animals are living things.

Living things grow and change.

They can have young.

living things

Nonliving Things

Nonliving things do not grow.

They do not change on their own.

They do not have young.

nonliving things

Environments

Plants and animals live in environments.

An **environment** is what is around a living thing.

It has what living things need.

flamingos in a wetland

A forest is an environment.

An ocean is an environment too.

wolf in a forest

shark in an ocean

Plants Have Parts

Roots hold the plant in the ground.

Roots take in water.

The **stem** carries water.

stem

roots

A **leaf** makes food for the plant.

Flowers make seeds.

Fruits have seeds.

flower

leaf

fruit

Kinds of Plants

Plants are different sizes.

Plants are different shapes.

Plants are different colors.

daisy

cactus

These plants are the same kind.

They both have fuzzy leaves.

But they are different colors.

pink petunia

purple petunia

Kinds of Animals

Giraffes are the same kind of animal.

How are these giraffes alike?

How are they different?

Some animals live in herds.

A **herd** is a group of animals of one kind.

A herd stays together.

herd of giraffes

Living Things Have Parents

A **parent** is a living thing that has young.

Plants can be like their parents.

How are these plants alike?

young plant

parent plant

Plants can be different from their parents.

How are these plants different?

young plant

parent plant

Animals and Their Parents

Animals can be like their parents.

How are these animals alike?

cow

calf

Animals can be different from their parents.

How are these animals different?

hen

chicks

Glossary

environment   everything that surrounds a living thing

herd   a group of animals of one kind that stays together

leaf   a part of a plant that makes food

living   things that can grow and change

nonliving   things that do not grow and change on their own

root   a part of a plant that takes in water

stem   a part of a plant that takes water from the roots to the leaves